W9-BZX-143

History Makers

Winston Churchill

...and World War II

Sarah Ridley

SEA-TO-SEA
Mankato Collingwood London

This edition first published in 2013 by
Sea-to-Sea Publications
Distributed by Black Rabbit Books
P.O. Box 3263, Mankato, Minnesota 56002

Printed in the United States of America,
North Mankato, MN

9 8 7 6 5 4 3 2

Published by arrangement with the Watts
Publishing Group Ltd, London.

Library of Congress Cataloging-in-Publication Data

Ridley, Sarah, 1963-
  Winston Churchill and World War II / Sarah Ridley.
    p. cm. -- (History makers)
  Includes index.
  ISBN 978-1-59771-393-1 (library binding)
1. Churchill, Winston, 1874-1965-- Juvenile literature. 2.
Prime ministers--Great Britain--Biography--Juvenile
literature. 3. World War, 1939-1945--Great Britain--Juvenile
literature. I. Title.
  DA566.9.C5R543 2012
  941.084092--dc23
  [B]
                              2011049886

Series Editor: Jeremy Smith
Art Director: Jonathan Hair
Design: Simon Morse
Cover Design: Jonathan Hair
Picture Research: Sarah Ridley

RD/6000006415/001
May 2012

Contents

The Churchill Family

Winston Churchill was born on November 30, 1874. His father was an English lord and his mother was a wealthy American.

Winston was born at his grandparents' home, Blenheim Palace, near Oxford, in England.

1837 ▶

Queen Victoria takes the throne of England.

Winston's family home was in London. His father was a Member of Parliament, and both his parents lived very busy lives. Winston did not see much of his parents, but he did grow very fond of his nanny.

A photograph of Winston's father, Lord Randolph Churchill.

Childhood

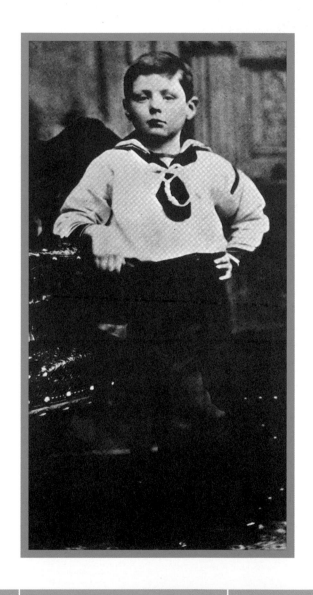

When Winston was four, the family moved to Ireland. A few years later, there was a new baby brother for Winston. His name was Jack.

◀ Winston as a young boy.

1877 ▶	February 1880 ▶	June 1880 ▶
The Churchill family moves to Ireland.	Jack Churchill is born.	The Churchill family returns to London.

Jack and Winston, on either side of their mother in 1889.

At the age of eight, Winston's parents sent him to a boarding school. He hated it. After two years, he moved to a different school. There he took an exam to go to a famous school called Harrow, and passed.

1882 ▶

Winston goes to a boarding school.

1887 ▶

Queen Victoria's Golden Jubilee.

From School to College

The teachers at Harrow School praised Winston's work in English and history. They were not as pleased with his arithmetic, or his timekeeping.

▲ Winston in school uniform. He missed his parents when he was away at school.

1888 ▶

Winston starts at Harrow School.

Winston in his army uniform.

Winston decided he wanted to be a soldier. After leaving school, he went to army college and he did well. Now he began his first army job in India.

1893 ▶

Winston starts at army college (called Sandhurst).

1895 ▶

Winston leaves army college. His father and his nanny die.

9

Adventures Abroad

Britain ruled over a huge empire that stretched around the world. The British army helped protect the

Empire. As a soldier in India, Winston was part of this.

Winston was a cavalry officer, a soldier on horseback.

1896 ▶

Winston goes to India.

After India, he went to fight in Sudan. Alongside his army life, Winston earned money by writing newspaper reports and history books.

▲ Winston took part in the Battle of Omdurman in Sudan.

1898 ▶

Winston goes to Sudan. The British army win the war there.

1899 ▶

The Boer War begins in South Africa.

Into Politics

After a few more adventures abroad, Winston decided that he wanted to be a politician. In 1900, he became a Member of Parliament (MP).

▶ In 1908, Winston married Clementine. They had five children.

1900 ▶
Winston becomes a Conservative Member of Parliament (MP).

1901 ▶
Queen Victoria dies. Edward VII is crowned.

1905 ▶
Winston becomes a Liberal MP.

Winston made one big mistake during the war, which resulted in thousands of soldiers dying at Gallipoli in Turkey.

In 1914, World War I started. During the war, Winston did some important jobs in the government and fought as a soldier for a short time.

1908 ▶

Winston and Clementine marry.

1910 ▶

Edward VII dies. George V is now king.

1914 ▶

World War I breaks out.

The Family Home

When World War I ended in 1918, Winston continued working as an MP. He shared his time between London and his country home.

Winston enjoyed building walls. Two of his children, Sarah and Mary, are helping here at their home, Chartwell, in Kent.

1918

World War I ends.

1922

Winston and Clementine buy Chartwell, a house in Kent.

During the 1930s, Winston began to worry about a man named Adolf Hitler who was gaining power in Germany. Winston feared he would start another world war.

Adolf Hitler became the leader of Germany in 1933.

1924 ▶

Winston changes back to the Conservative Party.

1933 ▶

Adolf Hitler becomes the German Chancellor.

World War II

In 1939, the German army invaded Poland. This led to Britain and France declaring war on Germany. The next year, Winston became the British Prime Minister.

▲ Winston gave many speeches on the radio and thousands listened.

1936 ▶

George V dies. Edward VIII is briefly king, followed by George VI.

1939 ▶

World War II begins.

British soldiers wade into the sea from French beaches after the German invasion.

The war was not going well for Britain. Germany had invaded several countries, including France. Winston gave speeches and worked long hours to inspire the British people to keep fighting the Germans.

May 10th
1940 ▶
Winston becomes Prime Minister at the age of 65.

1940 ▶
Germany invades many countries.

May 26–June 4
1940 ▶
British troops are rescued from Dunkirk, in France.

17

Battle of Britain

Some German airplanes during the Battle of Britain.

In the summer of 1940, Hitler ordered the German air force to bomb British ports and airfields. For three months, the Royal Air Force fought the Germans and beat them.

June
1940 ▶

Italy joins the war on the German side.

However, Hitler could not be stopped that easily. He gave the order to bomb British cities instead. He wanted to make Britain surrender.

1940 ▶

The Battle of Britain. The British and German air forces battle in the air.

1940-1941 ▶

Air raids on British cities.

War Around the World

In 1941, Russia and the United States joined the war and battles raged around the world. Winston kept the British people strong, even when the news was bad.

▶ Winston flew around the world to encourage British soldiers and sailors.

1941 ▶	1942 ▶	1944 ▶
Russia and the United States enter the war.	Japan wins many battles.	D-Day Landings. A million U.S. and British troops invade France.

After five long years, the war ended in 1945. Germany had lost. Now the British people wanted a change, and Winston lost his position as Prime Minister.

Winston waves to the crowds on the day the war ended in Europe.

June
1945 ▶
World War II ends.

July
1945 ▶
Winston is replaced by Clement Attlee as Prime Minister.

June
1947 ▶
India gains independence from Britain.

21

Last Years

Winston became Prime Minister once more in 1951. After four years, he left this job but he remained a Member of Parliament almost until his death.

▲ Winston enjoyed painting while on vacation, and at home.

1951 ▶	1952 ▶	June 1953 ▶
Winston becomes Prime Minister, age 76.	George VI dies. Elizabeth II becomes queen.	Coronation of Elizabeth II.

London came to a halt as Winston's coffin was pulled through the streets.

In old age, Winston traveled, wrote books, painted, and spent time with his large family. He died in 1965 at the age of 90. Remembered as one of the greatest British leaders, his funeral was watched by millions.

December
1953 ▶
Winston wins the Nobel Prize for Literature.

1955 ▶
Winston resigns as Prime Minister.

January 24th
1965
Winston dies, at the age of 90.

23

Glossary

Air raid A bomb attack from airplanes.

Boarding school A school where children live during the semester.

Cavalry Soldiers who fight on horseback.

Conservative Party One of the main political parties of Great Britain.

Coronation When a king or queen is crowned.

Golden Jubilee The celebration held to mark 50 years of a king or queen's reign.

Hitler Adolf Hitler was the leader of the German National Socialist (Nazi) Party.

Liberal Party One of the main political parties of Great Britain.

Member of Parliament A person elected by voters in the UK to represent them in the British House of Commons.

Nanny Someone paid to look after the children in a wealthy family.

Prime Minister The leader of the government of Great Britain.

RAF The name given to Britain's Royal Air Force.

World War I The world war fought between 1914 and 1918.

World War II The world war between 1939 and 1945.

Index